SHANNELL G. GRIGGS

This Was Her
A Poetic Reflection

To Ms. Pam
You are an amazing spirit.
I'm excited about our new
Friendship !

Love always,

This book is based upon the real-life experiences of Shannell G. Griggs. The author assumes all responsibility for inaccurate portrayal of events or activities that may be questioned or deemed factually incorrect.

For Mature Readers.

THIS WAS HER

TABLE

Dedicated especially to:
My Grandma Essie Lee Duhart
My Grandfather Hezekiah Griggs Sr.
My Great Aunt Sister

MY
BEGINNING

"You just licked the nastiest part of my body". Those words keep playing over and over in my head. She knew it was wrong I didn't but she let her pleasure block my innocence and that selfish decision will be a part of my every decision for the rest of my life. Sherman street second floor bedroom by the large window, full size bed, pink and white beddings, beautiful china mirror, and television lights flickering sound on low. My eyes didn't see any of that just a smell of vagina- A smell I wouldn't know existed for years to come but I did my job that I had to do. She told me she needed me and that would help her-shoot even then at 4 years of age I always lend my helping hand to those in need and it was taken for weakness and advantage of. Our lips connected and that's my memory of a first kiss. Her chubby fingers rubbing my vagina sucking what little

breast I had and telling me I was hers. I will always
be a cheater now.

INNOCENCE

BEGAN

This is my beginning
This is the start of a brand new
ending.

The ending of the beginning to my
many life spells.

The ones that had me cursed into
the secrecy of the truth inside me.

Looking in the mirror and seeing
the death as the reflection of my
impression to my minds
confessions of confusion.

I don't understand miracles of
things meant to happen. My
beginning is the ending to
everlasting living.

So I wait patiently in the pastures
deeply covered in life's garden.

The sun will shine and I'll have my
light to bloom and be merry. Have

my heart I don't love no way.

But my mind will stay.

I have to think of colors blue,
white, red – without mind I'm
brain dead – can't live.

Heartless people live breathe and
become victorious take my heart.

They ask when will your life
begin?

I say it's when you judge me no
more when I cry no more when
this world no longer gives up light
no more. When it ends is when I'll
begin.

This is *my* beginning. The start of a
brand new ending. The ending to
no more, no, no more,

To those who wait…

I THOUGHT SHE - just wanted to spend the night. But I would do what she needed as long as she didn't wake my little big brother who slept in the bed right next to us. Her left hand on my head the moans from her vocals letting me know I'm doing a good job-a sound I wouldn't know the meaning of until years later but I did my job I had to do-shoot even then at 4 years of age I always lend my helping and to those in need. Hair in my mouth my innocence in her vagina and her poison in my body. I had to come up for air ok! I was being smothered! I had to go to bed! If my mom came back from downstairs where she took that cardboard shelf like thing with her to play cards in the little green car parked out in front, only on the nights she needed her medicine. She had to have her medicine. Didn't your mother need her medicine from that little green car that was parked out front of your house? Mommy are you there? where are you? I can't breathe! She says why did you stop. Something in that moment told me it wasn't right. But she let me know I just licked the nastiest part of her body, and she would let me know for the rest of my life. My life ended that night.

TRAPPED

Her

How you rob her of *her* innocence?
How could you rape her of her tomorrows?
How could you be so selfish and forget about her sorrows?

Now her days are filled with sadness. Her love is wicked and her heart burnt. She didn't care about the little girl who would be left hurt.

When she was four is when it all began. Always sneaking in the bed next to her feeling between legs creating new wounds sexing her.

Robbing her first time, taking her first choice, not caring who or what she wanted silencing her screaming voice. She was robbed of her innocence. How could you rape her of *her* tomorrows?

How could you be so selfish and forget about her sorrows?

When she opened her mouth they said: 'shut up with the lies.'

She wipes her tears and kisses *her* sex life good bye.

She can't look in the mirror can't love herself.

Being insecure
– unsure of who she wants –
becomes herself.

Now she's 10, and *she's* 16, still the same scene still touching her sticking fingers in holes.

What she was thinking one could never know.
She was robbed of her innocence.
She was raped of her tomorrows.

How could you be so selfish and not care about her sorrows?

That girl had enough issues to deal with that was known.

Little missy was a child, but, *her*

lifestyle was grown.

Her mom was gone for the time being because the streets knew her name.

Her dad was left in the streets if they were there she would have no shame.

All she wants is a *sorry for what was done* to her soul so she can rebuild the life that a person stole.

She can move on and live a normal life be *something* to a husband *they* call a wife.

But she hides in sorrow, the midst of pain, all the silent thunder and misty rain.

She was robbed of *her* innocence.

Raped of her tomorrows *that* girl was selfish and didn't care about **my** sorrows.

THE PAIN

Dear Diary *(entry 170)*

I remember when I was a little girl being hungry. I could still hear my mother's voice I could see the despair in her eyes. It's like I could see her truth although she lied to her soul. I knew we weren't going to starve anymore. "Nell put on your shoes get your book bag." I always lend a helping hand to those in need even if the pity was on me. We walked to the supermarket and filled my book bag with food. Being hungry and not relying on school lunch for a meal because we didn't go often began to take a toll on us. Walking through that door with that book-bag full of food was like someone gave us a free ticket to be happy. Happiness never came without an invite. What was in my little school book-bag to a bunch of hungry kids was equivalent to a supermarket. That's when being humble became a way of life, being thankful for having just enough, being greedy I could never understand. I always wondered how my mom got through those rough times, she made sure we were full before she even thought about lifting a fork to get a bite to eat. That's something I would always respect my mother for. As a woman she starved herself for her children. I wish my mom knew how strong she truly was. So discussing this with her and seeing she's in a better place lifts my heart. I do love my mom and I'm happy I realized this now before it's too late. I told her the absence really affected my life. Today she apologized for everything. So how can I not accept? I went months almost a year without speaking to my mother or seeing her. I don't want that with us. I just want us to learn to love each other. I know I'm going to try. How cool will it be if I could just pick up the phone and call her just to see how she was doing? I'm excited thinking about the possibilities. I want that mom back that use to be so much fun and entertaining. It wasn't always bad. I am going to love her because she is my mom. It took a long time to get this point. I remember her telling me my name came from a woman my father cheated on her with. It made me feel like that was the reason I felt she didn't love me. Why did she leave me then ? That was my mindset as a little girl always thinking about "why".

Happy Mother's Day

Your mom may have said don't do drugs while sitting on your bed giving you a hug

My mother used it from January to December she showed me to make sure I would always remember.

Your mother told you my mother showed me.
She lived her life through constant tragedy just to show me how not to be.

Your mom probably told you to love yourself and respect who you are, my mom living without a soul showed me to love me her greatest gift by far.

Your mom may have said and for that you love her in a special way, my mother showed me everything through imagery and for that she's the greatest mother in the world in this poem
today!

HUMBLE

I Feel Your Pain

I feel your pain; I see your gain.
I know heartache and I know
muddy waters through the rain.

Lightning crashing, love is
hurting.

Leave to stay here contemplating
hurting yourself because of others
actions of time.

Fearing truth through world
discoveries is the crime.

My people be strong don't ever
give up live blue.

Don't be told things from your
heart which isn't true. My peoples
blame my people's shame, pain
and *pain*.

My people's pain.

The Shadows

Don't hide behind the shaded
dreams of *hope*

People wear masks because the
shadows show more than a dark
spot on the ground. Even that
shows the artistic expression of
bullshit.

Don't hide behind the shaded
dreams of hope, even the blind
can see they too know left from
right.

It's those who trick the wise into
feeling sorry for those who were
never sorry to begin with.

Take my hand and walk with me.

Let me show you what's behind
the writers painting.

What was covered by the image of
imagination – feel his creation the

demonstration of yet another beauty a *beauty* instigating the truth. The vibrant feeling of laughter with pain.

Tears are not always salty – follow me on this journey to discover all the amazing inspirations that inspired them to believe – to create a *Real-Life* behind bars figuratively spoken to identify lack of freedom because society says you can't be who you want to be anymore.

I take back hope and bring life to memories of the future not the past.

I don't hide behind the shaded dreams of Hope people wear mask because this life they can't cope.

Inspire. Dream. Hope. Believe. Imagine and Create.

Love

Makes you smile.
Makes you laugh.
Makes you jump for joy.
Makes you cry.
Makes you frown.
Makes you fall broken.

Love is a complex, and
unorthodox.

Don't forget love is beautiful and
also a deception.

By far the greatest contradiction
of all time.

The hurt isn't the side effect
of love because during the
breaking and crying someone is
still loving the pain.

Will you continue to love?

MY TRUTH

I guess what bothered me about my mom is she always tells me stories of her childhood. Everything my Grandad did for his family. I use to be so envious. My Grandad is a great man. He was always the life saver. I know for a fact if he knew all we truly went through he wouldn't have it. A lot of things were kept a secret. My Grandad is a strong man. A loving man in his own way. My Grandad is one of the greatest men I know. No matter what time of day you call he'll answer. He's always there. When I was young we lived with him until he sold his house and moved down south to Alabama. What if he never left? What if we left with him? Life could be different. I wish we never separated. I love you Grandad.

When my brother and I were separated my granny filled the void in my heart, and she became my new best friend. I admired her love for God, and the hope she had for the possibilities to come for our family.

With my granny by my side, I never gave up. She respected me because even though I was only eight-years-old she saw a survivor in me.

With my mother nowhere to be found, I had to learn how to survive on my own. I had to use my situation to the best of my ability. I learned how to lie, and I took on the responsibility of handling some of the important responsibilities in my granny's house.

The time I spent living with my granny was necessary for me. I knew she loved me, and although she couldn't do much, I was her heart. I will always love her for that.

FRIENDSHIP

Dear Diary *(entry 32)*

Today I feel horrible. I disrespected the one person who means the world to me, my granny. I can't believe I raised my voice at her. Even though I still feel she is wrong for what she did it still gave me no right to talk to her the way I did. I remember when all I had was my granny it was us against the world. She was my best friend and my diary. Before I didn't have to write anything down I could just tell her. I remember for whatever reason I was left with my granny and it was us. I at an early age I had to sacrifice my childhood to make sure we both were good. With her being disabled in a wheelchair we had to help each other. I could remember walking up a long hill just to get to the food store so we could have food to eat. I was washing clothes, cashing checks, cooking and helping my grandmother take care of me. I remember my 4th grade picture was hideous; I'm laughing just thinking about it. I had to wear one of her old dresses and a pair of her old shoes when she was up and walking. She tried her best to curl my bangs and put my hair in a ponytail. lol all I can remember is her hands shaking. My hair looked horrible but we tried and that's all that mattered. When I look back at things now I wonder where everyone was. To be honest there was no way I was going to leave my granny. I loved her too much. Even if my mom was to come back for me I would have stayed with her. Who was going to take care of her the way I could? Who was going to know what she liked to eat? Who was going to help her upstairs? Who was going to eat dinner with her? So you know what I did I kept my mouth shut about everything and it all was our secret. I could never lose her. I love my granny. I have to call her now. Better yet I'm just going to go over to house. I'm sorry granny.

LOVE

Her Words

What *she* said made me feel this way. The love the effect on my mind will always stay. A mind so in tune with wisdom and peace. Leaving an everlasting impact on one soul to release her heart speaks through *her* eyes and her mind thinks through *her* mouth.

She embodies truth, courage and intellect raised from the south. Experience she has her hair shows the triumph of a life her feet tell a story of blood danger and strife she is history her story tells it all her hunched over walk, the cane used to not fall.

The fire in her eyes the desire in her ears, to listen and speak. To live and give life. My heart saddens because she can't stay.

Her words what she said made me feel this way.

Dear Diary *(entry 45)*

Today I rode pass my great grandmother's house. Man I miss her so much I wish she was here to see me now. I wish I knew her at this age I need her. She doesn't talk to me anymore. When she passed away I took it really bad. My whole family did. Looking at her house today I swore I could see her sitting in her favorite window. I was her little lady and going to her house to stay the night was the best times. She always did what she could for me. I miss her. I'm going to go get some flowers for her grave. She would always come to me in my dreams it's like she was trying to tell me something. I guess I didn't get the message and she got tired of trying because I don't dream of her anymore.

LEGACY

I Am

I am courage in an Army of destruction
with no purpose or heart.

I am life in the dead living souls who
don't want to be here. No heart just
body parts. I am the light that strikes
the eyes in the sunniest day.

I am the bravest in a battle with no win
but I came to fight anyway. I am beauty
when you feel like the mirrors are all
cursed.

I am the mysterious *money appeared* to a
woman trying to feed her children that
she finds in her purse.

I am hope and faith and everything you
wish for.

I am here to save you but *you* are too
afraid to open up and let me through
your door.

- To those who are weak.

MY
STRUGGLE

THEY CALLED ME names so I hated going to school. Every day I was afraid someone was going to notice my hair wasn't done or my clothes were dirty.

I started hating myself. I wanted to be someone else so that I wouldn't have to deal with all of my problems.

I hated being light-skinned because I thought if I was darker no one would notice me.

Maybe I would be beautiful darker?

All of my brown-skinned friends had everything you could think of. I thought being light-skinned was the reason I went through so much.

Eventually the teasing became numb to me.

At least I'm not being bullied or beaten up.

I knew I was supposed to be thankful despite it all.

Dear Diary *(entry 72)*

I saw an old classmate today who made my life a living hell in school. He wasn't the only one that teased me but he always took it too far I mean everyday he was picking on me. Seeing him out there in the streets looking horrible made me feel bad for him. I know what he did to me wasn't right but we were still children. He use to have the nicest clothes it just seemed he had it all. I wondered what happened to him. I swear if I ever decide to have children I'm going to teach them to be humble. Never tease someone because of what they don't have. Kids can be cruel and maybe that starts at home. We are all equal no matter the fancy clothes we dress up in. When we were younger everything is done by our parents or guardians. But when we become adults that's what matters most what we can do for ourselves. If you are going to judge me base it off of me being adult when I am able. I still feel bad for him hope he gets it together. I'm going to pray for him.

Reflection

I understand how it feels to be teased. I know how it feels to be talked about because of the things you don't have. To those of you who are still going through this please don't let this stop your growth. Your future is not based off what you have right now. Once you get to that point where you can have what you want and be who you want, what people thought of you won't matter. It's hard going to school and trying to hide because you don't want people to notice you. I was quiet most of the time because I was tired of being on the radar. At an early age I had a heavy complex about myself. I hated my skin color. I wanted to be everyone else. It took years to look at myself and realize I am who I am and I'm not going to change. Love yourself. I know the pain of not having certain things. Please don't give in and give up. That person teasing you now could be the one you have to help in the future. I have overcome that humiliation you will too. You are beautiful and material things don't make that word come true. I love you!

Unchangeable

I am who I am and I'm not going
to change

I am who I am and I will remain
the same you always try to change
me into someone I'm not and quite
frankly it has to stop

Love me or leave me but don't try
and break I'm tired of living a lie
I'm tired of asking God why

Why you can't just love me for the
person I was made into always
telling me what I should do

How I should wear my hair or the
clothes I wear well I'm here to tell
you that I really don't care

I don't care if you don't like me
I don't care if you try and fight me
I don't care if you try to break me
down and I don't care if you scorn
my name all around town because
for too long I was made to believe
that you were right for me

For too long I was made to believe
you was who I wanted to be

I'm so glad I see things clearer and
so glad I've been drawn nearer

Nearer to self-respect nearer to self
esteem

Nearer to everything I should have
been loved about me

You covered my eyes and filled
them with so much hate

It was my fault I was weak and it
made me easy bait but I'm so
happy that I found where I stand
with my head held high looking
over this land so forget you
negativity and yea it's like that go
away and I pray that you never
come back!

"to those who struggle with what
others say"

Motivation

I would rather be who I am naturally than to try way too hard to be something I'm not.

Before you can love yourself, find out who you are and discover the true meaning behind your smile the true meaning why you frown.

Look into your eyes and discover the endless possibilities of the power bestowed upon you.

And for once tell *them* who you are; it matters not what they think.

Drifting off in my daze, fantasizing of what could be, I could hear life calling me saying run away come and go with me.

Run away Shannell, become someone else nobody will know.

I didn't see the beautiful, loved, smart girl people said I was. I saw shame and ugliness.
I began to hate myself and my total existence. It's like my life was a movie and every time the tape started rolling someone just messes it up and magically changes the ending.

SADNESS

MY CRY

Dear Diary *(entry 101)*

Today I had my sister drop you off to me. I missed writing in you and I'm sorry if I disappointed you in any way. Last I wrote to you I said I wasn't going to hurt myself. Now I'm here in this hospital explaining to everyone why I did what I did. I just had enough I no longer wanted to live with the pain. I felt alone and empty. I always felt like garbage pick-up sometimes worst because eventually that gets picked up. I was deep in my sorrow and shame and didn't think I could ever get back up. I made the decision to leave this world this thing "they" call life. I was in a dark place and I felt unsavable.

I need to be saved from God too once again but this time from flesh someone here who i can see touch feel smell maybe one day he will come and pick me up out the pot hole filled with water everyone keeps driving over that's where I reside well in my head at least I feel like an old lady who from the looks on her face is tired of being here I want to be saved from that person to come whisk me away I felt like a princess story but it didn't match up because my life isn't fairy tale so I'm more unsavable maybe my knight will come because my eyes get big or maybe he will hear my laughter or maybe he'll just come because he saw me laying in the pot hole filled water but for now I'm unsavable.

So all I saw was those pills that I bought. I crushed them up and took as many as my body could stomach. I thought I was dead I was in a dream so real that I felt true peace. I woke up and I felt the pain of the tubes down my throat and the pain in my stomach. Waking up seeing the living I knew I had a lot of explaining to do. I just want to get out of here and go back home and finish my duties in the military. I guess I need to learn how to live. This isn't my first time trying to leave God must be trying to tell me something. I'm hungry though and want to eat some real food. Can't wait to leave here and get my hair done and see my granny and tell her I'm sorry for what I've done. Got to go and get ready for group talk to you later.

HELP

Reflection 1

When I tried to commit suicide and it was unsuccessful I felt so much shame. I was embarrassed. Some people started calling me crazy. I felt like I was back to being a child getting teased. I didn't know what was worst the feeling before I tried or after. I knew I had to put my past away for good so i can live but I felt I had too much weight. It took a while for me to discuss this situation but I am no longer ashamed I know that tomorrow is a brighter day and can't worry about the ones who don't understand why I did what I did. I worry about the ones like me going through the severe depressed feeling of not wanting to live.

Reflection 2

Depression is a serious disease and I want those to know who struggle with it that I feel your discomfort. I too suffer from it but with counseling and surrounding ourselves with positivity life can be lived to your norm. Don't worry about what people have to say about you through this struggle. Live for you and fight for self. If you feel you don't have the support from friends or family, there are tons of programs to help you. Just make the first step and someone will walk with you the rest of the way. You are not alone. You are only alone around those who don't understand you. If you are on the other side and you know someone suffering from this disease be careful with your words. If you can help them try but if you can't don't be so cruel. You are not pathetic! You are not a coward! You are not searching for attention! You are crying out for help. I once had to live for someone so they wouldn't be hurt. Trust me you are loved think of those who love you. So, please I love you and need you here so LIVE FOR ME! Someday you will help someone and they will be here another day because they will live for you. We are all human and have different feelings.

June Reflections

June 1st
Take my hand lead me to the
endless possibilities for you and I.

Give me what I'm worth and
never short me my time for I have
overcome the hurt others have
selfishly given to me.

Not caring about what my heart
can take what it has already
endured.

Waiting for someone is like
waiting for God to come back.
Only with God you can depend on
his word.

People change like blue skies
turning grey showering on your
pain built in from the radiant sun.

Too much can harm but too little
the flower cannot blossom.

Like the earth won't move if I'm

standing on it. Impossible.

June 5th

When I awake sometimes I ask
why?
Why even be put here another
day?
Why go through that hurt all over
again?
Why even be around to sing that
song again?

I believe I can make it through the
odds of even days to come.

Just as time heals the breaking
glass of misery filled cups that
have been spiked with unwanted
negativity from those who despise.
He who has gifts will always be
selfish with words to cure fallen
soldiers in the world.

But I wait till the day I awake in
the peaceful atmosphere never to
ask why.

What's it Gonna Be?

He couldn't live as who he wanted to be so he died as who he was.

She lived her life through constant tragedy like crack and coke sorry and pain was her drug.

They were used and abused walked and picked on. The only chance of living was living 2 be gone.

Society's gain on making us feel less than worthless seeing girls and boys take their lives is society's purpose we get fixed up and tripped up on a life some can't live to see. It's either us or society to defend so what's it gonna' be?

Dedicated to Suicidal Children. I love you if nobody else does!

My People
If you ever had to fight a battle
already lost just to prove you're
not weak this is for you my lovely
people.

Ever searched for peace in a busy
atmosphere yelling and fighting
but was still for peace this is for
you my people. My people.

Yesterday

My heart was ripped out yesterday.
My mind was so in tune with the
touch of love that my soul could
not stay.

To live for and die for something
isn't living for or dying for.
It is just being fooled into
believing that you can't just live
for self, you cannot just die for
self.

Let me tell you something about
yesterday.

It is *my* future not tomorrow.
Nor today.

You see it matters to my life and it
matters to my strife for yesterday
is when I died and today is my
afterlife.

I didn't like who I was, I could not
possibly take the pain of what
society tells me of inflictions I

have to gain.

My yesterday matters it is a part of me. To live to die so my soul can be set free.

Anybody going in the direction of my way I have to let go and relive my tomorrow's future through my yesterday.

MY
FEELINGS

Dear Diary *(entry 46)*

I miss my father. Today I stumbled across a picture of him and it filled with all kinds of emotions. I wish he was more involved in my life. I love him but the time we have spent apart affected my ability to see who he really is to me. I want to be angry with him I want to hate him for not being there. I wanted to be daddy's little girl and I feel he took all my childhood wishes away. I never knew at the time why my parents separated. What I can remember is that one day he wasn't there. I always wanted him to come back though, always wished he would come and rescue me. It's crazy when I think of me back then it was all about wishing now for me it's about praying. Giving everything to GOD and not the stars. Feels good to rely on something more concrete. I am no longer upset with him for the decisions he has made. He inspired me to write as well. My father is so intelligent. I just sit back in think of the fun times we shared. I wish he could have been more and done more. But his life is his life and my life is my life and I can't dwell on his path that he chose. Being older and seeing the truth it wasn't his fought he wasn't there. We lived in separate states. At least he tried his best to make the summers sweeter. I'm thankful though, Thankful that I can still love him. Although he wasn't around I would never search for another person to fill that spot. I hope one day I am able to tell him this. For now, I at least have this picture.

"As I sit back and stare at this 4*10 frame of a man who is strong healthy and confident I can hear him began to talk to me. He says I love you baby girl and I will always protect you. He looks like my father but this frame exudes a man in another realm of what you call a dad. In this frame, this man standing there beside my bed on my night stand gives me hope and courage. The man in this picture will do anything for his daughter. I am the princess in his kingdom. This frame right now is just a fantasy."

Reflection
Sometimes as women we search for a certain kind of love. Love from a man and if we don't receive it from home we may run wild and crazy giving

ourselves to anyone who seems interested. All our situations and reactions to things are different. I don't want us as women to feel like we have to give our hearts to someone who shows a little attention just because we lack a father figure at home.

Let's find out the root to why your dad wasn't there. Get closure so you can live a prosperous life without feeling used when you finally find someone who loves you. I'm thankful that I never ran wild and crazy. So to my girls, ladies, women if it helps use my words to guide you to a place where you don't have to fill a fatherless void with someone who is no good. Love yourself more and give yourself the chance first to love you. Trust me it's worth it.

STRENGTH

A Feeling

Finding life in a coffin 6ft under
what's breathing what's moving
just stop and wonder.

It feels like loving without a heart
having your brains split apart

But yet your still breathing

Living with no world seeing
without sight trying to forgive and
hate being the peacemaking while
starting a fight.

It's complex

Happy to be alive begging to die
eating in front of hunger watching
hungry children cry.

It's murder.

Can't even get up because I'm still
standing

Can't fall down
if I'm lying on the landing – It's a
natural cause.

I'm the darkness in the morning
the fear at 3 am. Braking glass in
the music headphones and I have
no life to spare. I'm without the
joy to learn to live.

The part of the sentence after but
the contradictory statement that
gets the mind stuck.

Rich in finance, unhappy for the
poor but can't give.

I am hope even though I need to
learn to live ...my thoughts

Why (Tupac's Song)

Why me? Why me? I ask God and
you know what he says:

*My child you are my messenger
through you others will change,
thorough you others will love,
through you people will see you can come
from nothing washed away by the sea.*

*I told Tupac
you are the rose that grew from concrete
People will fight harder and see through
you they can reach the sky.*

*SO my child, pain = success and that's
the reason why.*

The Crying Game

I cried my last tear like every day
this week.

If tears were blood I would be
internally ill.

If crying stopped poverty I would
have enough to put 100's of
families in homes a week.

I cry so much I forget to smile.
How to laugh? How to be happy?

All I know is tears and pain.

Loving over and over forgiving
taking back the same.

I'm over this crying game.

I want

I hear lullabies in the morning of
a childhood dreamed of; I feel
warm kisses at night from a father
dream of; I can taste sweet nectar
of love given to me from a family;

I can dream my last dream of a
peaceful time in memory.

Can I have some of that?

Yes, what I see you shining
around?

You away dance and jump about
smiles on faces never frown.

I love that girl my heart yearns to
know.

Fill my past with what you got so
I can have something to
remember through time.

Tickle my fancy, wipe away the

bloody waters of grime.

Huh? You say it's what given
from above?

Oh, it's that it thing out now
called love.

I sing lullabies in the morning to
my future child dreamed of.

He gives me warm kisses at night
my husband dreamed of.

To my little girls who want.

This was
SHANNELL

Sometimes life takes us through journeys so we can be stronger. This was just a glimpse into my world. This was the hardest thing I ever had to do but I feel it's necessary. Someone out there needed to hear a piece of my story just so they can start to accept theirs. I'm grateful I'm still here. Please don't ever give up! Love yourself and respect others. Help someone along the way. I've lost a lot. I've lost some friends, lost some relationships, even family. I realized that someone out there needs me. Someone out there loves me! Someone out there is living just for me so I can help them. I want to start a movement called Live for Me. Saving someone's life is key. If you live for me, I'll live for you and you just keep passing it along. I am only here because I had to live for someone, and I also saved someone's life. If you are reading this I just want to say

thank you for picking up this quick book of
mine and supporting me.
Shannell loves you!

PEACE

MY THANKS

FIRST GOD FOR FORGIVING ME

SPECIAL THANKS TO SGT RICHARD COHEN, THANK YOU FOR SAVING ME WHEN I THOUGHT I COULDN'T BE SAVED. BEING THERE FOR ME AT A TIME WHEN ALL I NEEDED WAS SOMEBODY. YOU LISTENED TO MY WRITINGS AND STAYED IN MY CORNER AND TOLD ME TO WRITE. I THANK YOU FOR GIVING ME THE CONFIDENCE TO LIVE OUT MY DREAM AND BEGAN TO WRITE THIS BOOK. THANK YOU FOR ACCEPTING ME INTO YOUR LIFE. I OWE YOU THESE WORDS. THANK YOU!

THANK YOU BRANDON COHEN FOR TELLING ME TO WRITE THIS BOOK. BELIEVING IT WOULD BE GREAT BEFORE I HAD A PARAGRAPH.

TO MY BEST FRIEND GIVONNI BUTLER AND HOPEFULLY MY FUTURE EVERYTHING. THANK YOU FOR MOTIVATING ME. THANK YOU FOR BEING THE ONLY PERSON TO

COME TO ALL MY SHOWS. THANK YOU FOR
BEING THE LOVE OF MY LIFE AND BRINGING
LIFE TO MY POEM UNSAVABLE. YOU HAVE
STOOD BY MY SIDE THROUGH THIS WHOLE
PROCESS. I AM BLESSED TO HAVE YOU. THANK
YOU

SHARON SANTOS WHO WAS MY MANAGER AT
WORK. THANK YOU FOR GOING THE EXTRA
MILE. THAT PHONE CALL SAVED THE DAY.

THANK YOU TO ALL MY SIBLINGS. SHAKEIS
SHAFON HEZEKIAH JALEEL KAHLIIA. I LOVE
YOU. JALEEL KEEP WRITING.

TO MY PARENTS THANK YOU FOR GIVING ME
YOUR BLESSING TO HELP ME TELL MY STORY.
SHARON GRIGGS. HEZEKIAH GRIGGS JR.

TERRELL MCDANIEL BECAUSE OF YOU I
STARTED WRITING. THANK YOU.
Your passion your talent had a great impact on my life. I
love you I'm so happy you opened my gift through yours.

THANK YOU GRANNY BEATRICE WILLIAMS FOR
BEING MY BEST FRIEND WHEN I NEEDED ONE.
THANK YOU FOR NEVER LEAVING MY SIDE
EVEN WHEN I GET CAUGHT UP IN MY LIFE.

To my grandparents Bennie Williams, Beatrice Williams, Gloria Armstrong, Rev. James David Armstrong. Thank you!

To my aunts specifically Shelley, Rene, Michelle, Robin.

TO EVERYONE WHO BELIEVED IN MY DREAM AND VISION.

TO ALL THAT BELIEVED IN MY WRITING. THANK YOU TO EVERY WHO CAME THROUGH MY LIFE WHILE ON THIS JOURNEY. THANK YOU TO MY FRIENDS AND FAMILY.

THIS WAS YOU!

This is your 30-day writing Journal

THIS WAS YOU

THIS WAS YOU

THIS WAS YOU

THIS WAS YOU

THIS WAS YOU

THIS WAS YOU

THIS WAS YOU

THIS WAS YOU

THIS WAS YOU

THIS WAS YOU

THIS WAS YOU

THIS WAS YOU

THIS WAS YOU

THIS WAS YOU

THIS WAS YOU

THIS WAS YOU

THIS WAS YOU

THIS WAS YOU

THIS WAS YOU

THIS WAS YOU

THIS WAS YOU

THIS WAS YOU

THIS WAS YOU

THIS WAS YOU

THIS WAS YOU

THIS WAS YOU

THIS WAS YOU

THIS WAS YOU

THIS WAS YOU

THIS WAS YOU

THIS WAS YOU

BREATHE

Made in the USA
Middletown, DE
10 October 2016